FIRST 50 BLUES TURNAROUNDS
YOU SHOULD PLAY ON GUITAR

by Dave Rubin

ISBN 978-1-5400-2850-1

Visit Hal Leonard Online at
www.halleonard.com

Contact us:
Hal Leonard
7777 West Bluemound Road
Milwaukee, WI 53213
Email: info@halleonard.com

In Europe, contact:
Hal Leonard Europe Limited
42 Wigmore Street
Marylebone, London, W1U 2RN
Email: info@halleonardeurope.com

In Australia, contact:
Hal Leonard Australia Pty. Ltd.
4 Lentara Court
Cheltenham, Victoria, 3192 Australia
Email: info@halleonard.com.au

INTRODUCTION

B. B. King once famously said, "The blues is simple music. Anyone can play it. But, would you want to *hear* anyone play it?" That resounding roar you just heard was not the levee breaking, but blues guitarists and fans in a voice of one shouting "No!" Many technical aspects of blues guitar go into playing the music "you want to hear," not the least of which are those that prevent all blues from sounding the same. Along with a variety of chord voicings and soloing strategies, near the top of the list would certainly have to be the use of the many turnarounds heard throughout the genre. The Rev. Billy F. Gibbons once sagely commented on how accurate pitch bending separates the authentic blues guitarist from the poseur. The same could be said for knowing a broad selection of cool turnarounds.

Following are 50 classic turnarounds shown in four different keys in standard tuning for the most practical application. They will add immeasurably to true blues street cred, while likewise contributing welcome harmonic variety to 12- and 8-bar blues progressions (as well as 16- and 24-bar progressions). All will want to hear them!

Performance Tip: As you work your way through the turnarounds, it will become apparent that not all of them are practical for every key. Choose accordingly.

Dave Rubin
NYC

Turnaround 1
Delta Blues I

Delta blues guitarists often played in the standard open keys of E, A, G, and D. In noisy, rowdy "jook" joints, unaccompanied solo acoustic guitar required open strings—which have the biggest, loudest sound—to cut through the din. Descending or ascending patterns particularly complement cut boogie accompaniments as heard in Johnny Temple's "Louise Louise Blues" (1936).

Key of E

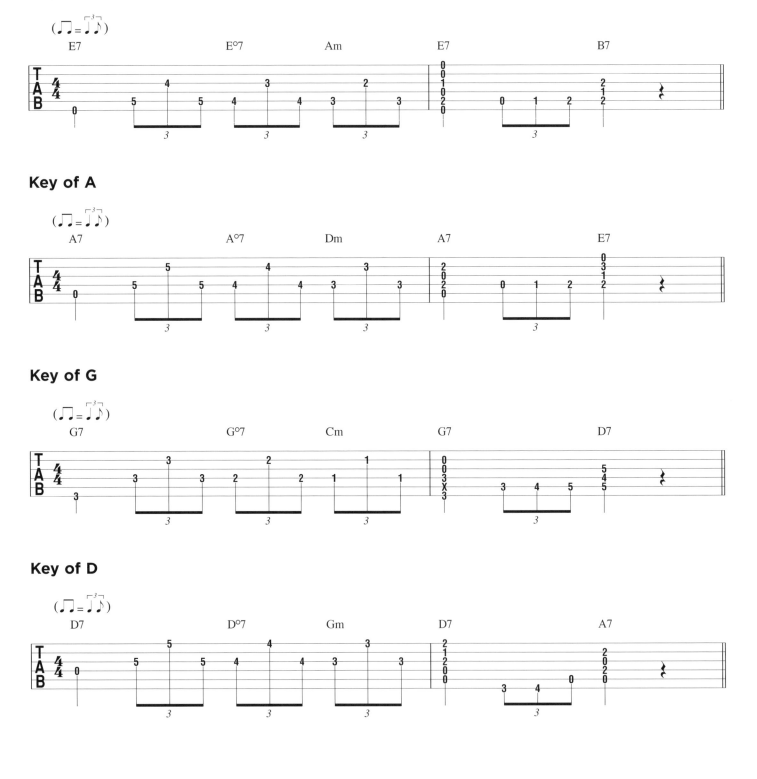

TURNAROUND 2
Delta Blues II

Johnny Temple's "Lead Pencil Blues" (1935) was the first recorded cut boogie blues. It had a profound influence on Robert Johnson for his "Sweet Home Chicago" (1936) and other classics, as he came to depend on a handful of descending turnaround patterns, including several that he used as intros. Notice how they can easily be transposed to all keys. Pick with your fingers or use hybrid picking (pick and fingers together) for these turnarounds.

Key of E

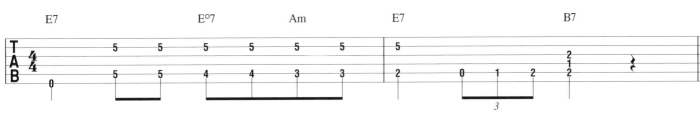

Key of A

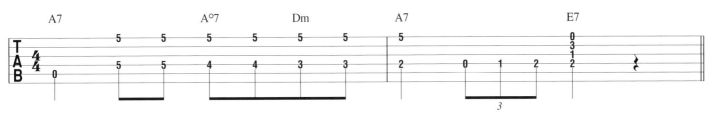

Key of G

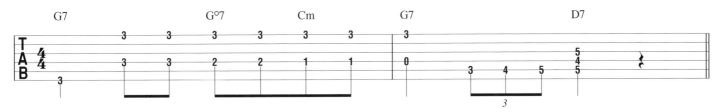

Key of D

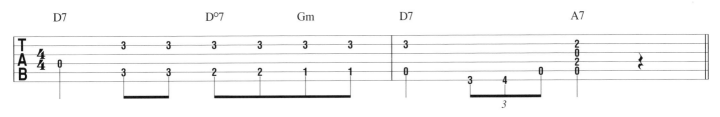

Turnaround 3
Delta Blues III

Dixieland jazz had a subtle influence on some Delta blues musicians, including Robert Johnson. His "Me and the Devil Blues," among his other compositions, contains a "jazzy" I–I7–IV–iv–I–V turnaround. The move from the IV to the iv imparts an expressive, melancholy feel.

Key of E

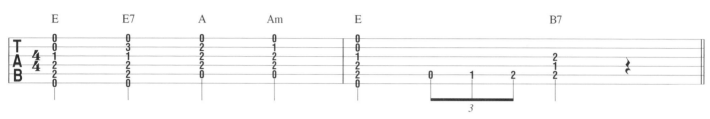

Key of A

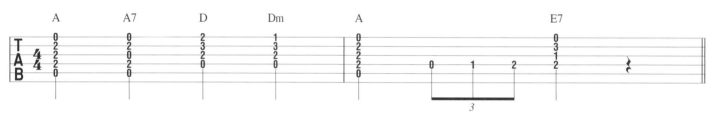

Key of C

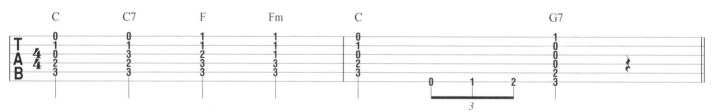

Key of G

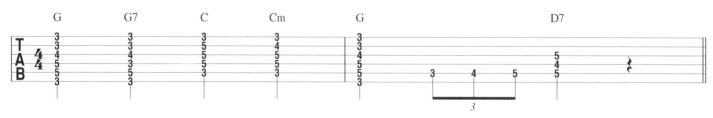

Turnaround 4
Delta Blues IV

The next examples utilize the top three strings of the open D7 chord form. This is a signature turnaround from the Delta blues of Robert Johnson leading to the Chicago blues of Muddy Waters. Similar to Delta Blues III, it also contains an implied iv chord.

Key of E

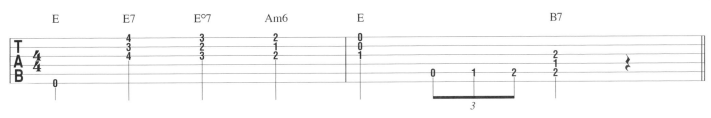

Key of G

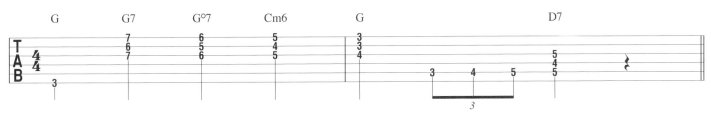

Key of A

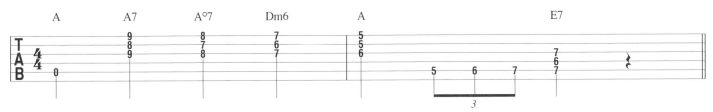

Key of D

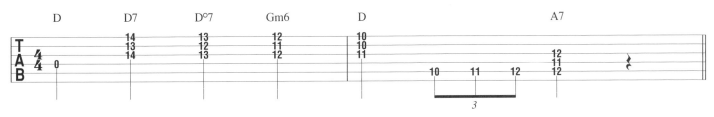

TURNAROUND 5
Delta Blues V

Note how this turnaround could easily be employed with slide when playing in standard tuning due to the descending patterns on the same frets. Pick with your fingers or use hybrid picking.

Key of G

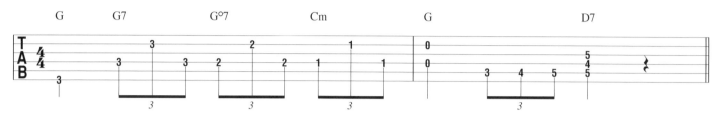

Key of A

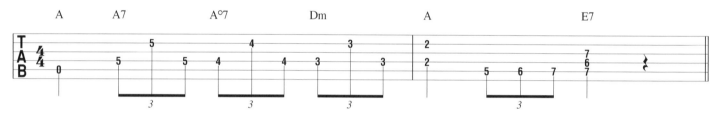

Key of D

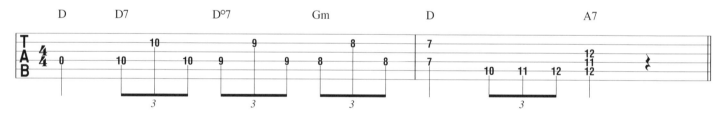

Key of E

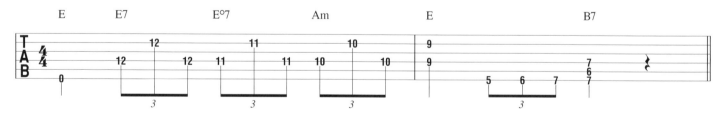

TURNAROUND 6
Delta Blues VI

Fast "train" or driving blues often feature stripped-down turnaround patterns that may be accessed quickly and easily. In addition, the bass-string riffs create an appropriate rumble.

Key of E

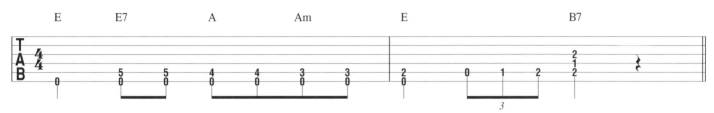

Key of A

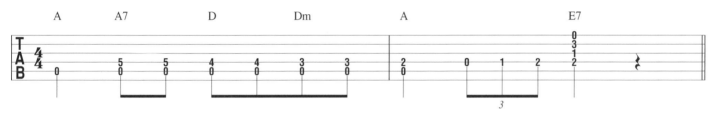

Key of D

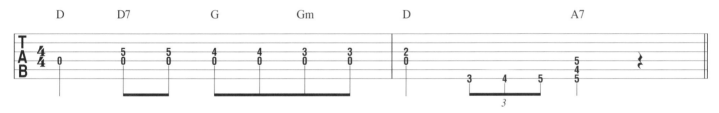

Key of G

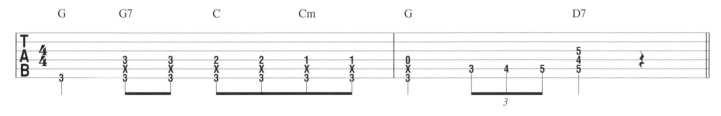

Turnaround 7
Delta Blues VII

In open tunings, turnarounds have common tones that make for smooth transitions between chords. However, it is possible to create the same effect in standard tuning, as can be seen here.

Key of G

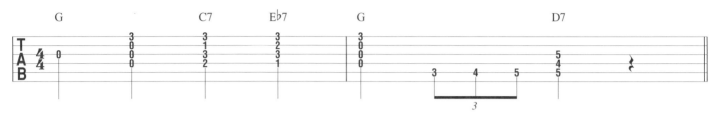

Key of A

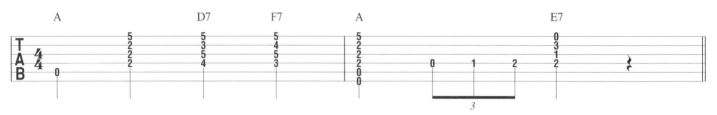

Key of D

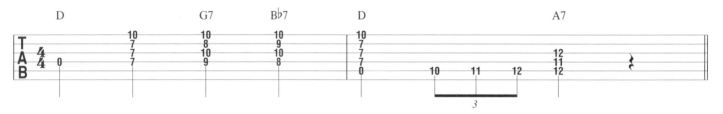

Key of E

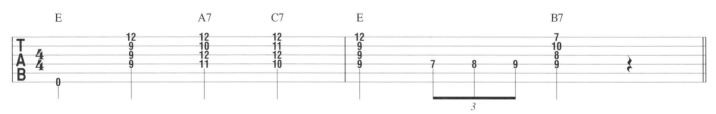

Turnaround 8
Delta Blues VIII

Many Delta blues guitarists, including the legendary "Robert Dusty," tended to choose from a relatively small group of turnarounds. Occasionally, though, they would break out this I–VI–II–V pattern.

Key of D

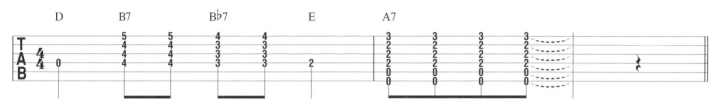

Key of A

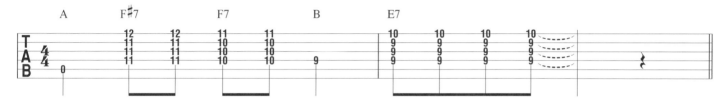

Key of E

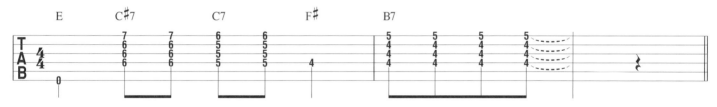

Key of G

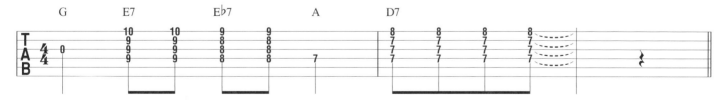

TURNAROUND 9
Delta Blues IX

Triplets are an essential element of many turnarounds and blues music in general. Skipping a string or strings, as in these broken chords, requires dexterity with a flat pick. Better yet, try hybrid picking or fingerstyle.

Key of A

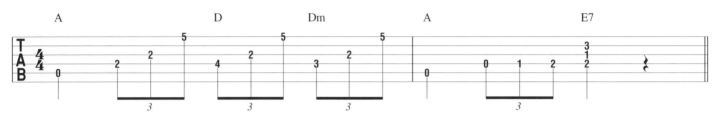

Key of G

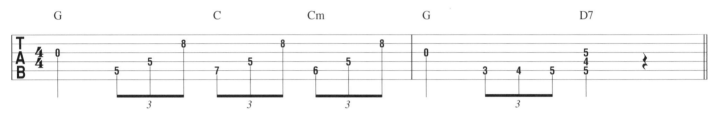

Key of E

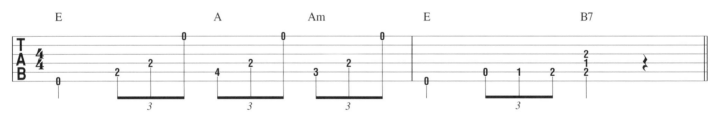

Key of D

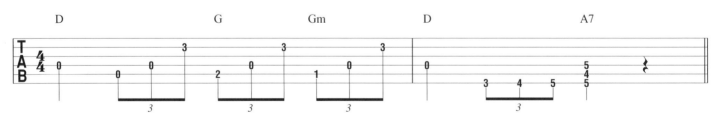

TURNAROUND 10
Delta Blues X

Again looking to the "King of the Delta Blues" for the last set of Delta turnarounds, an unusual but useful variation is presented. It is similar to "Love in Vain" because of its melodious descending 3rds.

Key of G

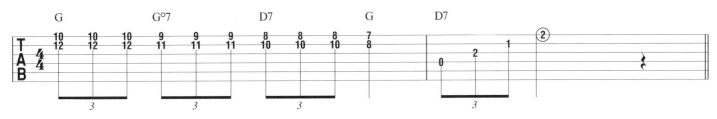

Key of E

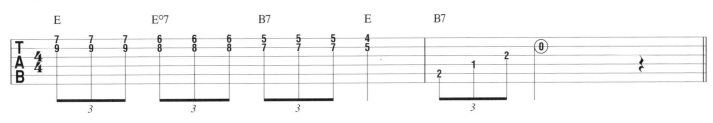

Key of D

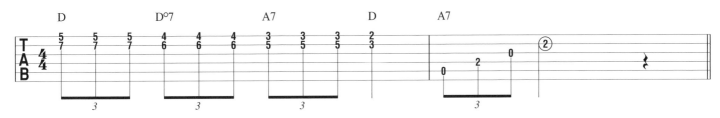

Key of C

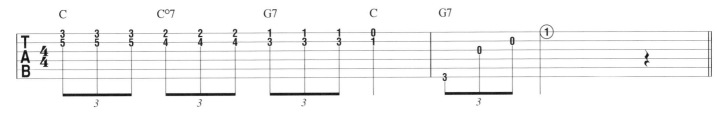

Turnaround 11
Piedmont Blues I

The late "Bowling Green" John Cephas, performing with his partner, harmonica ace Phil Wiggins, was one of the greatest modern proponents of the Piedmont blues guitar style. Though often sharing stylistic elements with Delta blues, Piedmont blues has more of a ragtime feel than a driving boogie or swinging shuffle feel. Use fingerstyle or hybrid picking for this example.

Key of E

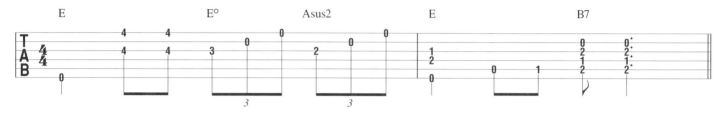

Key of A

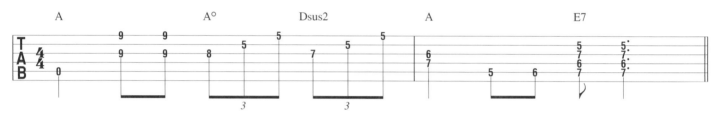

Key of G

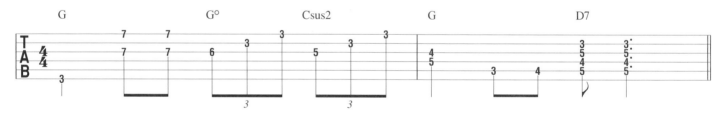

Key of D

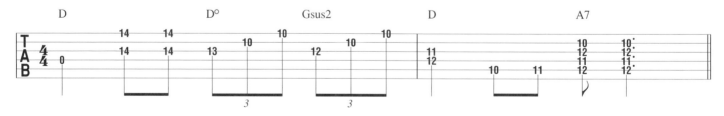

TURNAROUND 12
Piedmont Blues II

Sidestepping the more harmonically involved descending diminished patterns so common in Delta blues, the I–V change (which is the essence of most turnarounds) is portrayed here with a darker hue via the descending bass notes.

Key of E

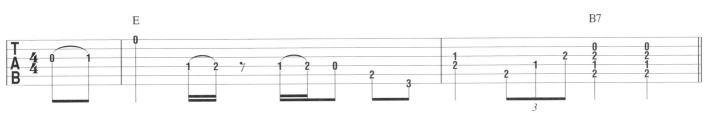

Key of G

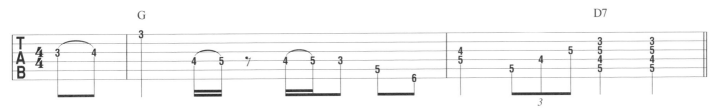

Key of A

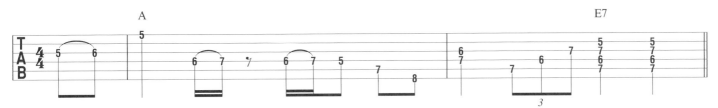

Key of B

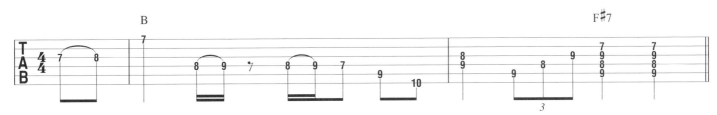

With so much Piedmont and ragtime blues in the key of C, it is essential to know a classic turnaround in the "people's key" as well as others. (Note: The example in the key of G shows the practicality of barre chords for certain keys; and because barre chords are moveable, you can play this pattern in any key.)

Key of C

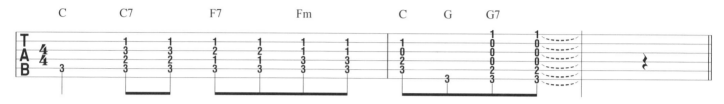

Key of A

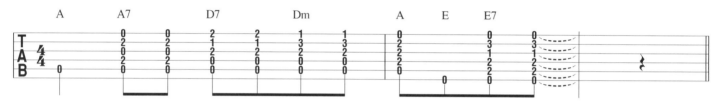

Key of E

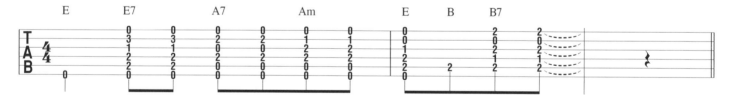

Key of G

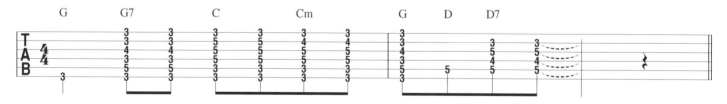

"Hesitation Blues" by the immortal Rev. Gary Davis has been covered countless times. The Hot Tuna version with Jorma Kaukonen on guitar and Jack Casady on bass helped to make it a modern finger-style standard. The turnaround for "Hesitation Blues" is one of the more harmonically sophisticated turnarounds in the blues, Piedmont or otherwise.

Key of C

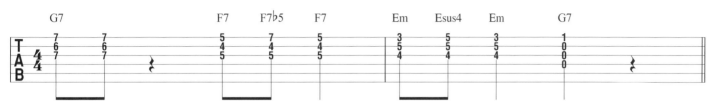

Key of D

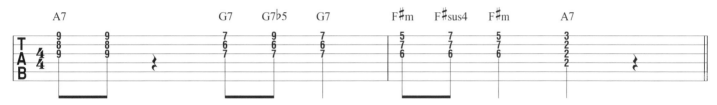

Key of E

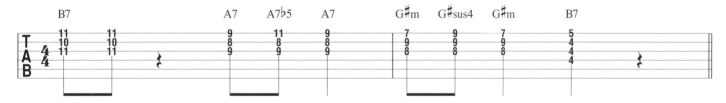

Key of G

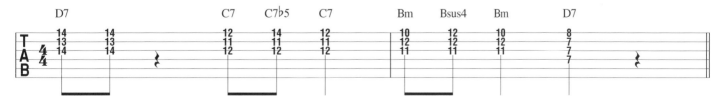

Piedmont Blues V

Carl Martin was a Piedmont picker not adverse to "swinging" rather than "ragging" his rhythms on occasion.

Key of E

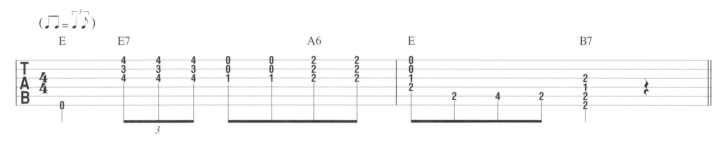

Key of G

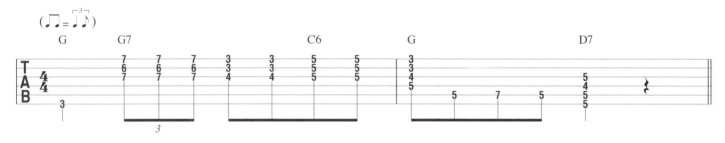

Key of A

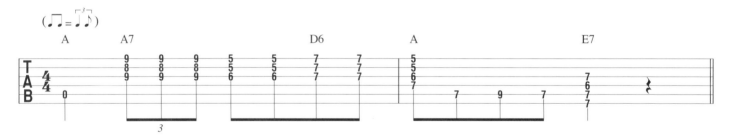

Key of C

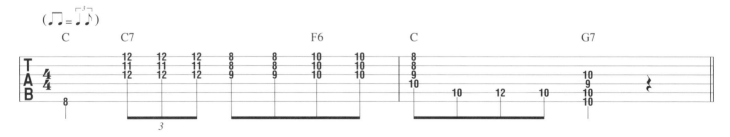

TURNAROUND 16
Piedmont Blues VI

Blind Willie McTell is one of the giants of Piedmont blues and prewar blues in general. He is most famous for "Statesboro Blues," though he composed many other renowned blues classics. McTell is justly famous for playing a 12-string guitar, but this turnaround sounds just as rich on a 6-string.

Key of C

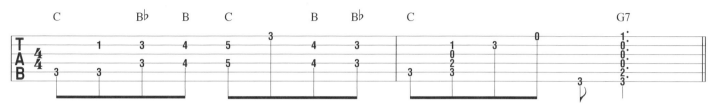

Key of D

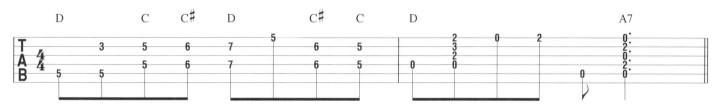

Key of A

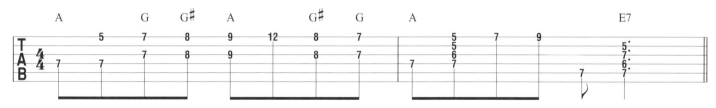

Key of G

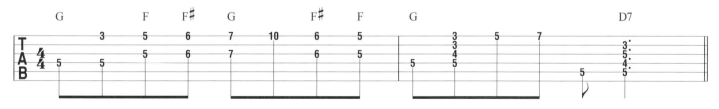

TURNAROUND 17
Piedmont Blues VII

McTell was a master of tasteful, fluid fills. Many are challenging, but some—like this spare turnaround—are quite accessible. Observe how the turnaround is not set up with the V chord but remains on the I chord to maintain momentum into, presumably, the next chorus of blues.

Key of A

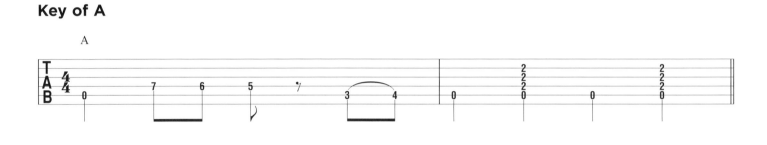

Key of D

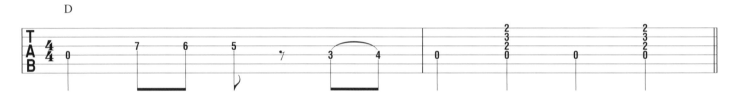

Key of G

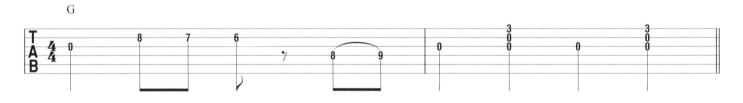

Key of E

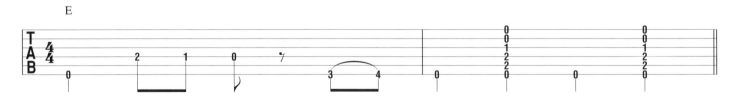

TURNAROUND 18
Piedmont Blues VIII

A sinewy turnaround riff from McTell illustrates his creativity with another "improvised" pattern. Be aware how, except for the ♭3rd (G in the first example) on beat 4, all the notes in measure 1 are in the Mixolydian mode, implying a dominant tonality.

Key of E

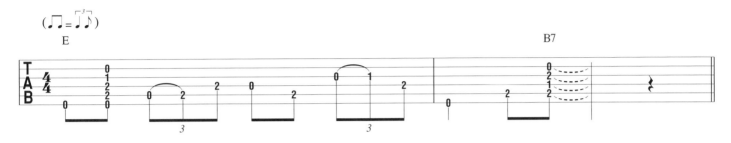

Key of A

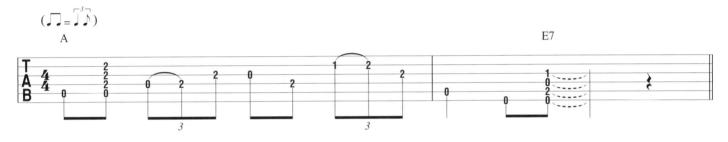

Key of D

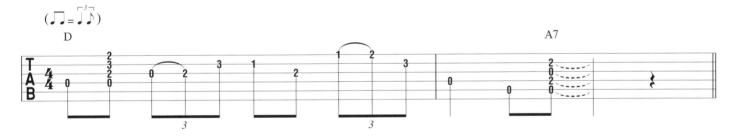

Key of G

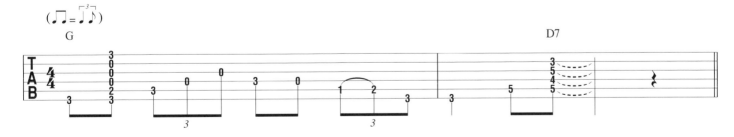

Turnaround 19
Piedmont Blues IX

Brownie McGhee, alone or with his longtime partner, harmonicist Sonny Terry, is one of the masters of Piedmont blues. Like a lot of blues, his music is deceptively simple. In measure 2 of the first example, check out how the first-inversion A chord (A with C# in the bass) adds one more descending bass step continuing from measure 1.

Key of A

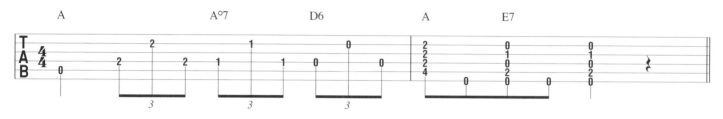

Key of G

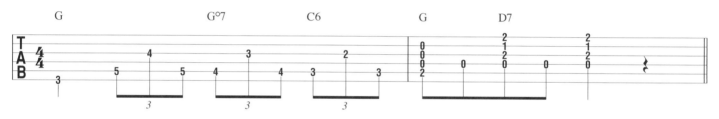

Key of D

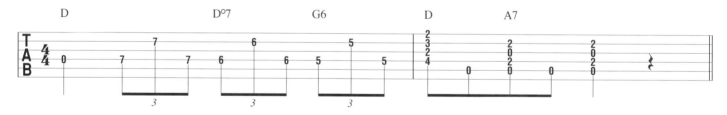

Key of E

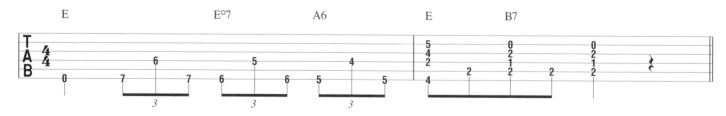

Turnaround 20
Piedmont Blues X

The last Piedmont blues turnaround shows how Brownie McGhee could be hip when desired, such as with this sly harmonic twist of the ♭VI chord in measure 1.

Key of A

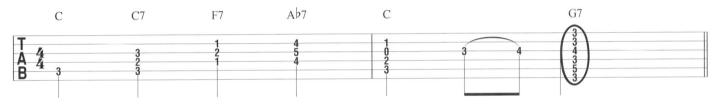

Key of C

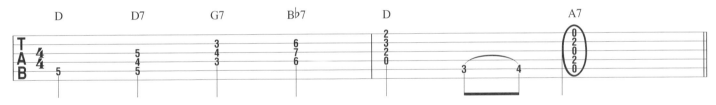

Key of D

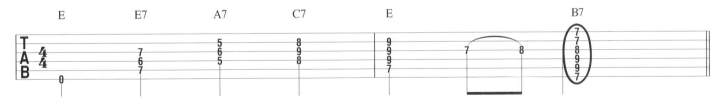

Key of E

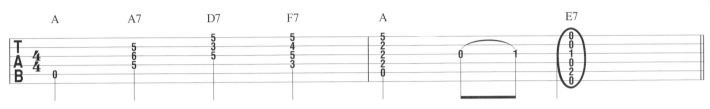

TURNAROUND 21
Chicago Blues I

A facile description of Chicago blues turnarounds would be that they are simply amplified versions of Delta blues turnarounds, and there is a grain of truth in that. However, the popularization of the electric guitar on the Chicago scene around the mid-1940s led blues guitarists to quickly grasp how the louder volume and robust tone could allow for new forms in the music. If not literally the first, Muddy Waters was certainly the most prominent of the postwar Chicago electric blues guitarists to realize the potential. His recordings from the late 1940s to the early 1950s changed the course of the blues, while also helping to pave the way for rock 'n' roll.

The first Chicago blues turnaround is essentially the ascending version of the first Delta blues turnaround that we covered. (Note: In "She Moves Me" and other Muddy classics, two guitarists play the ascending and descending patterns at the same time for a spectacularly dissonant effect!)

Key of E

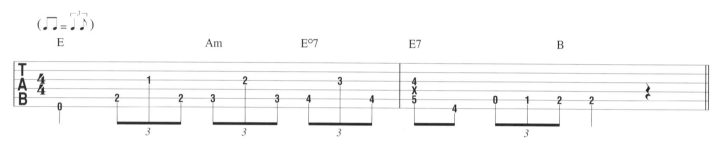

Key of G

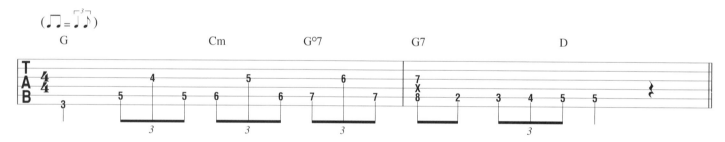

Key of A

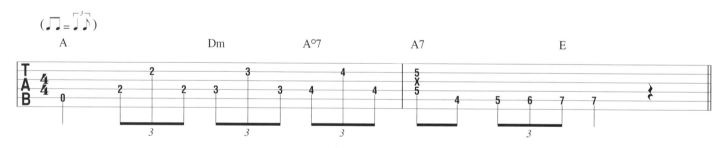

Key of D

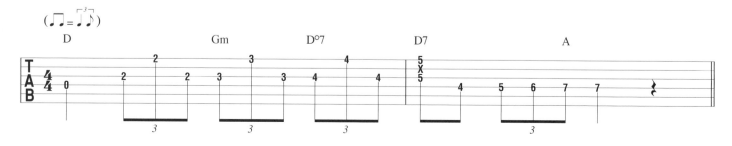

TURNAROUND 22
Chicago Blues II

Muddy pleads "Baby, please don't go" and proves the "less is more" dictum if hot vacuum tubes are at play. This turnaround is especially effective for up-tempo shuffles.

Key of G

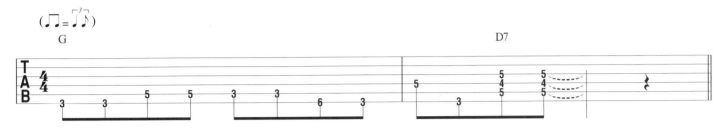

Key of E

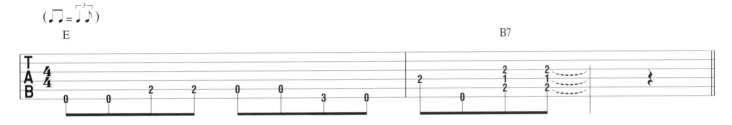

Key of A

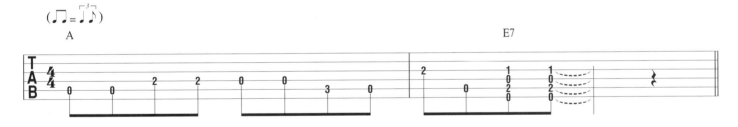

Key of D

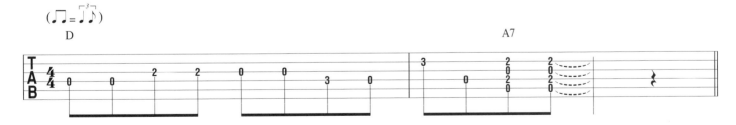

TURNAROUND 23
Chicago Blues III

Here's another fast shuffle turnaround with single notes climbing dramatically up the octave.

Key of G

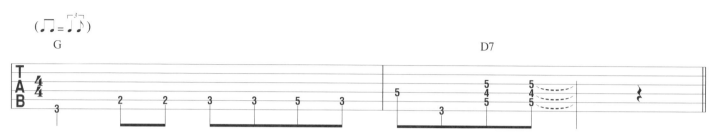

Key of E

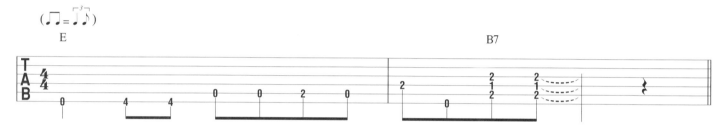

Key of A

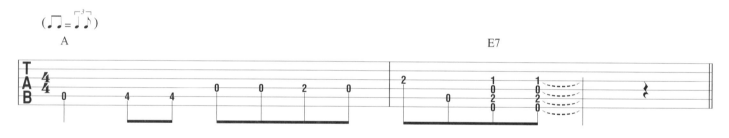

Key of D

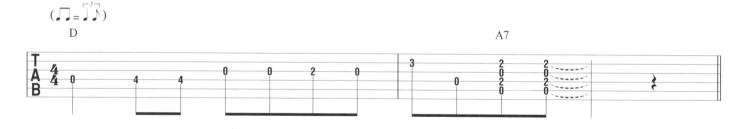

Turnaround 24
Chicago Blues IV

Thumping triplets compress the energy as the notes climb to the 5th on beat 1 of measure 2 and Muddy declares "Everyone knows I'm here!"

Key of A

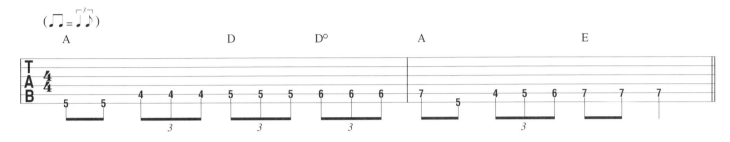

Key of E

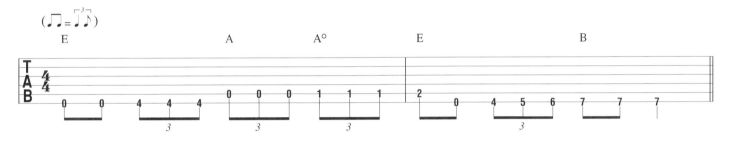

Key of G

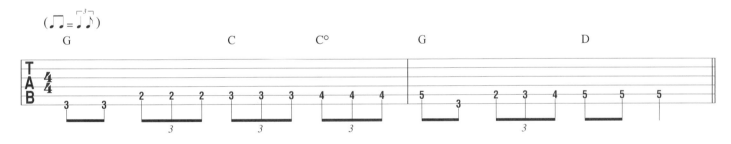

Key of C

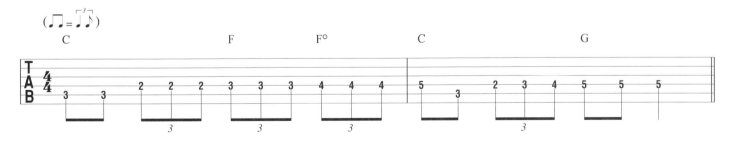

TURNAROUND 25
Chicago Blues V

The legendary Jimmy Rogers plays a lyrical lead turnaround that is "sweet" as "sugar" on a swinging Muddy shuffle.

Key of A

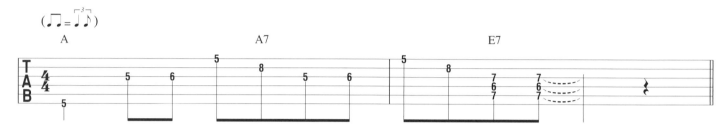

Key of G

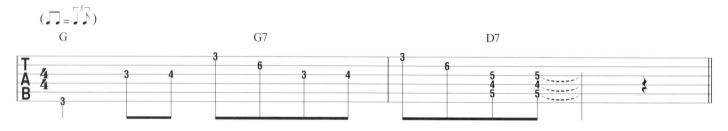

Key of E

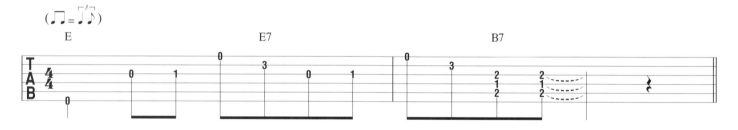

Key of C

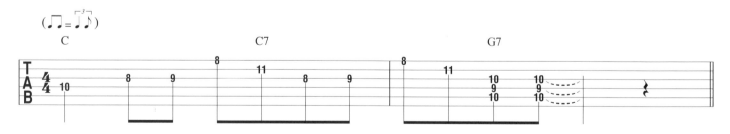

TURNAROUND 26
Chicago Blues VI

As hard-core blues fans know, Muddy and Howlin' Wolf enjoyed a friendly rivalry for many years, and it would be a brave soul indeed who would take an unequivocal stance on who was greater. However, a good barroom argument (or brawl) could be made that Wolf had the better lead guitarists pre-1970 in Willie Johnson and Hubert Sumlin. In this turnaround, Wolf is growling "Oh, Red," but he could have used his famous exhortation to Johnson to "Play that guitar till it smokes!"

Key of A

Key of G

Key of E

Key of C

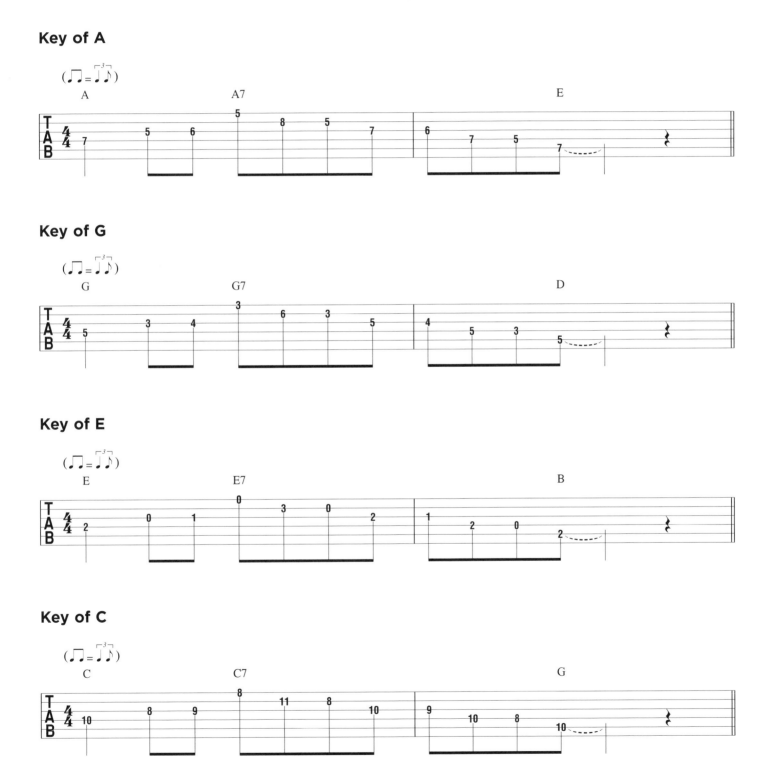

TURNAROUND 27
Chicago Blues VII

Taking a page from the T-Bone Walker playbook, Willie Johnson outlines the I–IV–I–V chord changes with deliberate restraint for a succinct musical statement.

Key of G

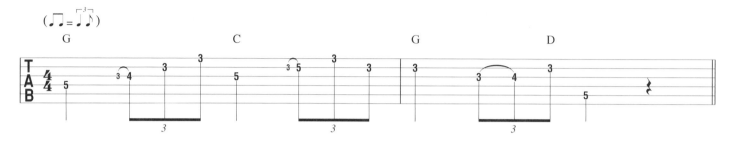

Key of A

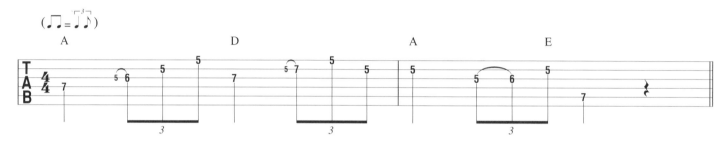

Key of E

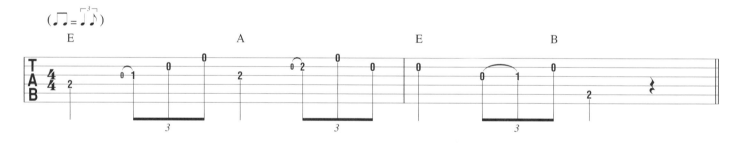

Key of C

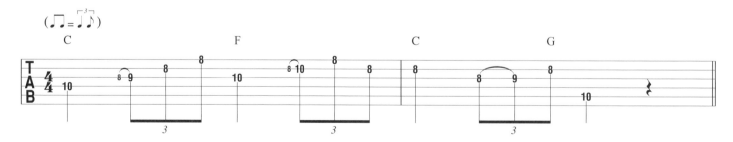

Turnaround 28
Chicago Blues VIII

When Jody Williams and Hubert Sumlin joined forces in Wolf's band in the early 1950s, they became a dynamic duo on a dream team that included Willie Dixon on upright bass and drummer Earl Phillips. Though still young, Hubert had awesome chops beyond others.

Performance Tip: Execute the quarter-step bend in measure 2 by pulling down with the index finger, except for in the third example (key of E) where string 3 is open.

Key of G

Key of A

Key of E

Key of C

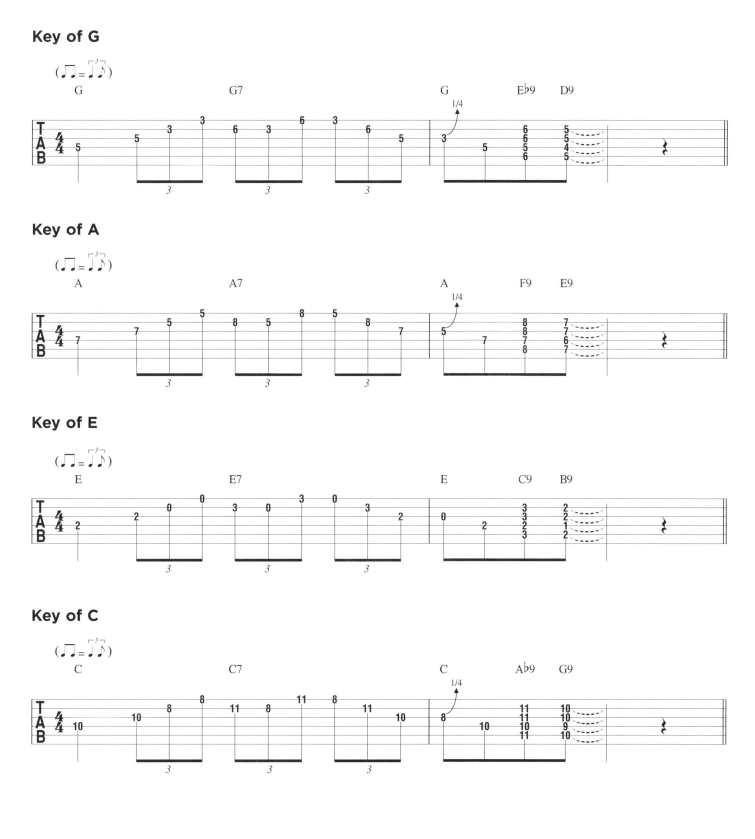

Chicago Blues IX

Transplanted Mississippian Elmore "Elmo" James epitomized postwar electric slide guitar. The classics he recorded (in standard tuning) with ace sideman Eddie Taylor are part of the granite foundation of electric blues.

Performance Tip: Use either the bare thumb and index finger or hybrid picking.

Key of D

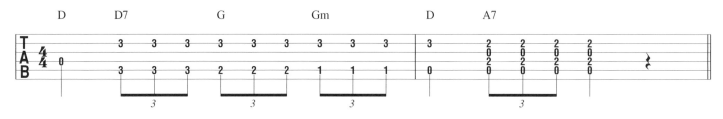

Key of E

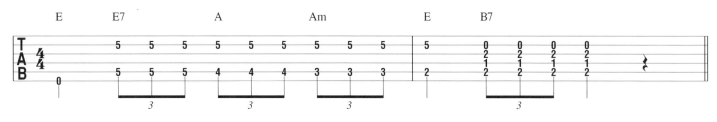

Key of A

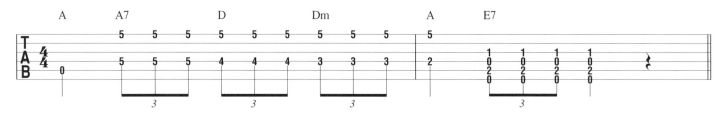

Key of G

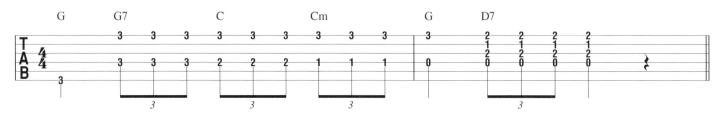

TURNAROUND 30
Chicago Blues X

This lead turnaround, as simple and graceful as it gets, is courtesy of Eddie Taylor, who could play many notes when called upon. Observe how the E and G notes relate to both the E (I) and A (IV) chords in the first example (key of E); this relationship can be seen in the other keys as well. In a fast shuffle and in conjunction with a second guitar strumming chords, this approach is very effective.

Key of E

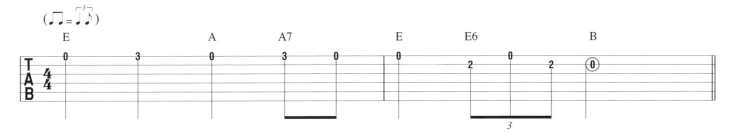

Key of G

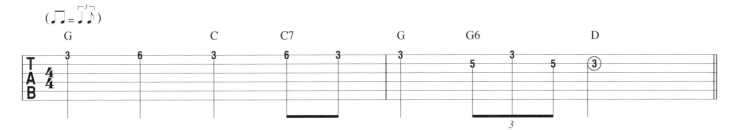

Key of A

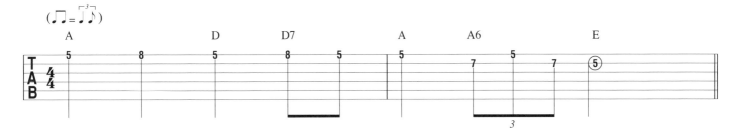

Key of C

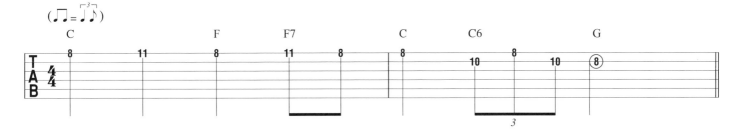

TURNAROUND 31
Texas Blues I

Blind Lemon Jefferson and other "tall" Texans preceded Sam "Lightnin'" Hopkins. However, Hopkins is the legend who created a personal prewar acoustic style and then moved forward in the 1950s with blazing, amped-up rockabilly before throttling back as time went by. Here is one of his classics when he ruled country blues in the open key of E.

Key of E

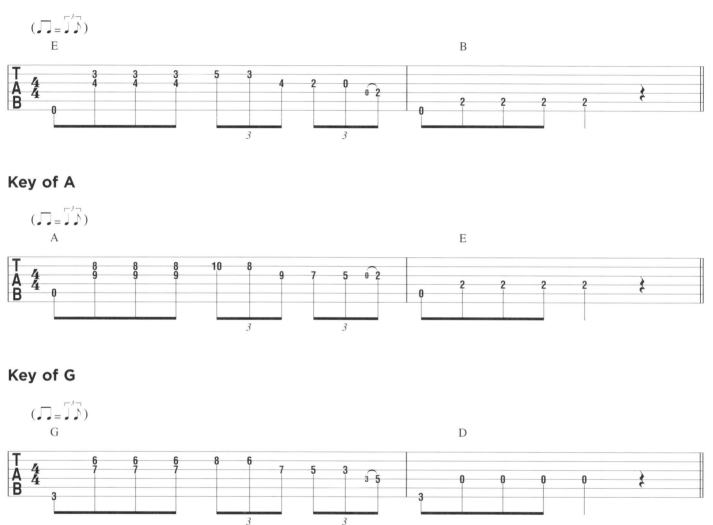

Key of A

Key of G

Key of C

Turnaround 32
Texas Blues II

The key of A in the open position was another of "Po Lightnin's" favorites.

Key of A

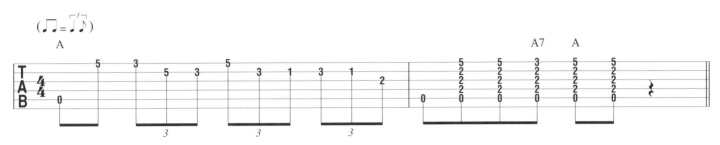

Key of G

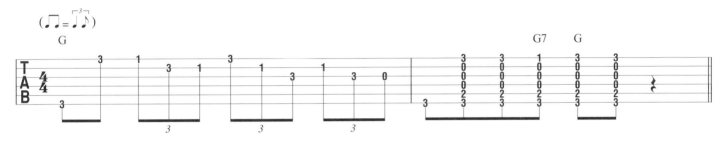

Key of E

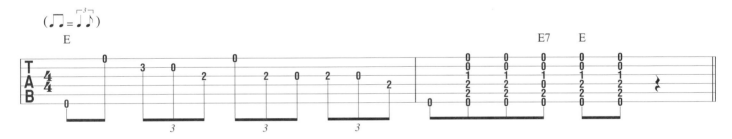

Key of C

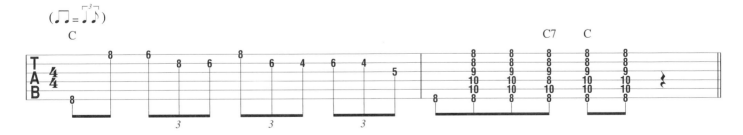

Turnaround 33
Texas Blues III

Though an example of the "less is more" axiom, Lightnin's slippery phrasing in these turnarounds gives the impression that much more is actually occurring on the strings.

Key of E

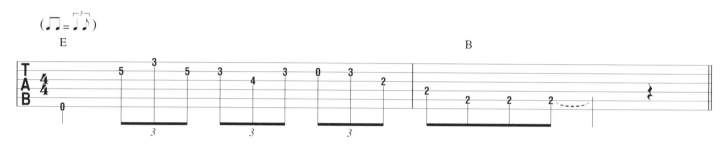

Key of A

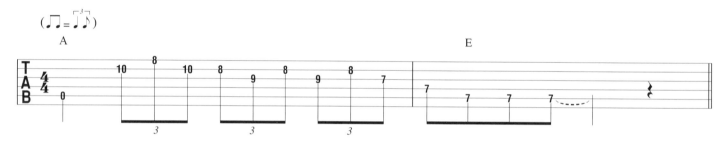

Key of G

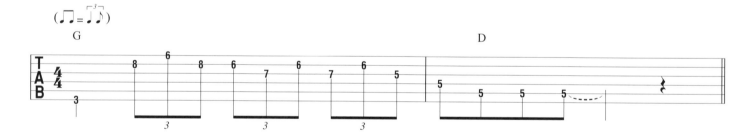

Key of C

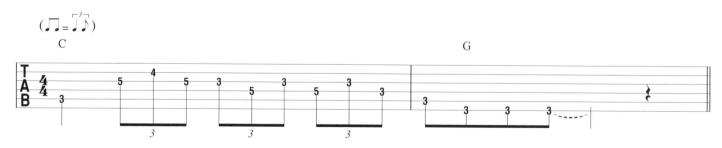

TURNAROUND 34
Texas Blues IV

Perhaps borrowing a page from the primal blues guitar book of John Lee Hooker, Lightnin' picks out a menacing bass-string turnaround that remains on the I chord rather than moving to the V chord. Pick with your bare fingers for an authentic sound.

Key of E

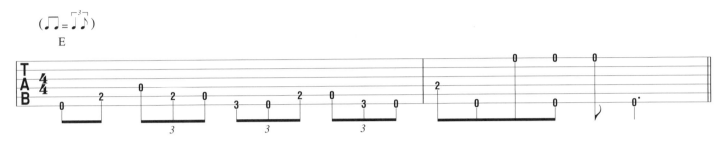

Key of A

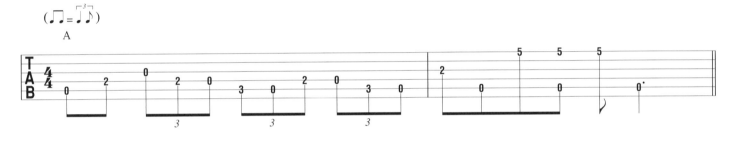

Key of G

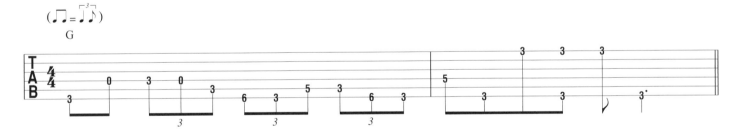

Key of C

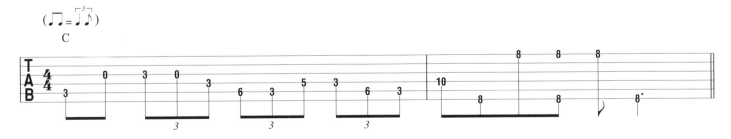

Texas Blues V

Freddie King was arguably the greatest Texas electric blues guitarist, and as such, his repertoire of turnarounds was second to none. The repeated motif in measures 11–12 of his most well-known instrumental is as iconic as any of its choruses.

Key of E

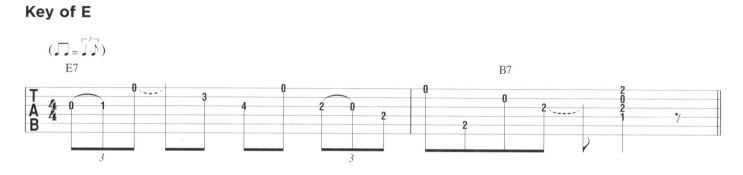

Key of G

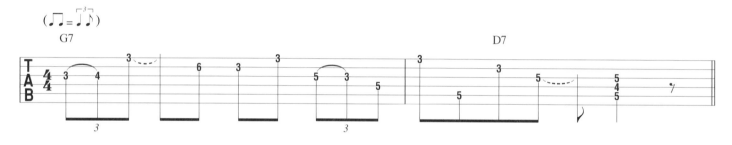

Key of A

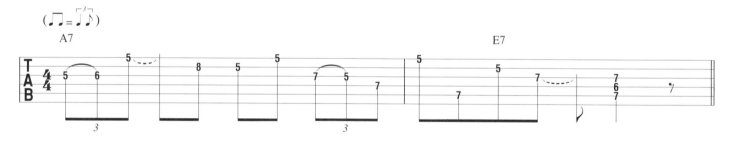

Key of C

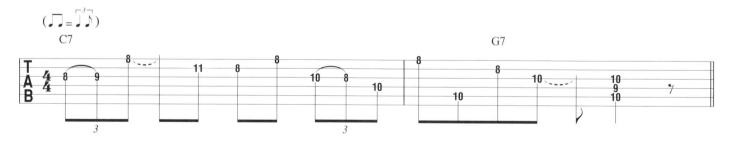

Turnaround 36
Texas Blues VI

Get "down" with another of Freddie's classics, virtually all of which contain memorable turnarounds that should be archived for future use!

Key of D

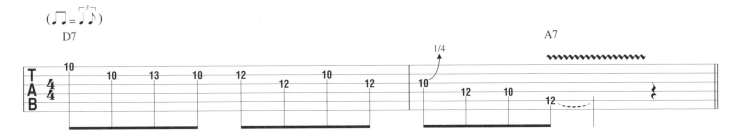

Key of C

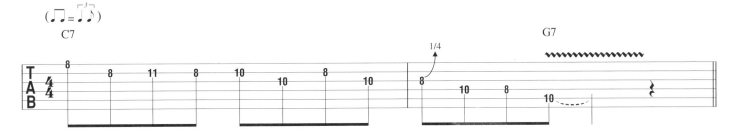

Key of A

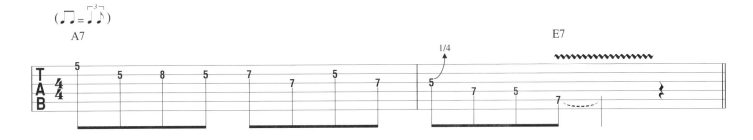

Key of G

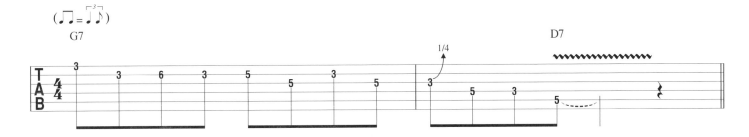

TURNAROUND 37
Texas Blues VII

Double stops, or dyads, play a prominent role in Freddie's instrumentals. The 3rds add harmonic weight in his musical tribute to a northern California city later made famous by Dionne Warwick. Notice how the turnaround stays on the I chord instead of moving to the V.

Key of C

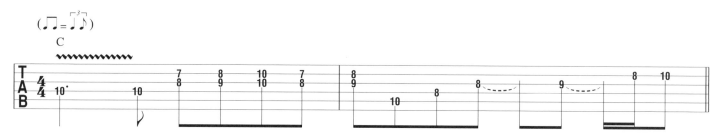

Key of A

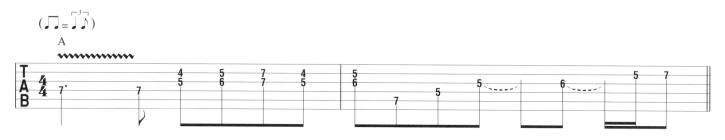

Key of G

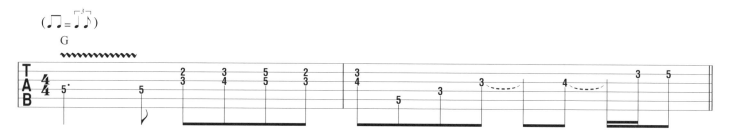

Key of E

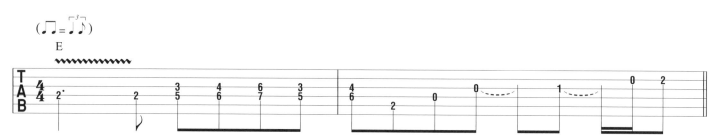

TURNAROUND 38
Texas Blues VIII

Freddie was right on track with this swinging romp up and down the G blues scale. He also includes a crucial major 3rd over the I chord in measure 1.

Key of G

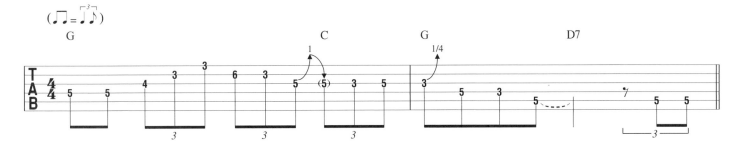

Key of A

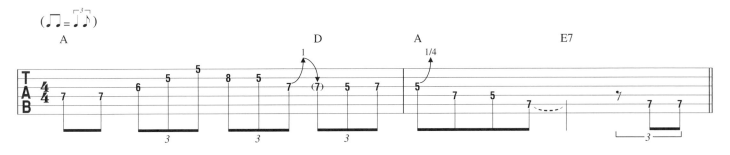

Key of C

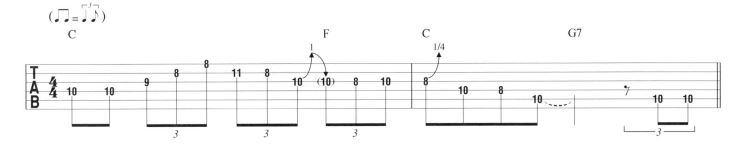

Key of D

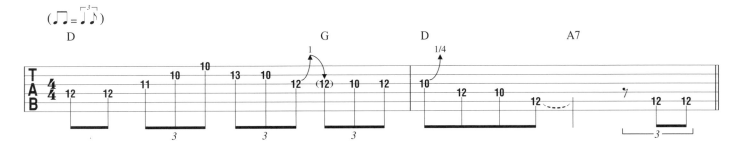

Turnaround 39
Texas Blues IX

The late, great blues virtuoso Stevie Ray Vaughan (1954–1990) was exceptionally creative with his improvised turnarounds. Many are crammed full of challenging, sizzling sixteenth notes. This one is more programmatic while showing cool, intelligent choices, especially with the descending C7 arpeggio in measure 2.

Key of C

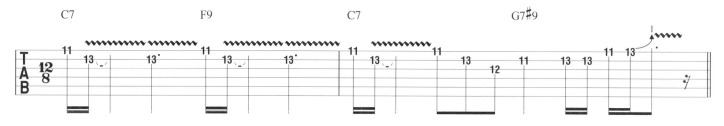

Key of D

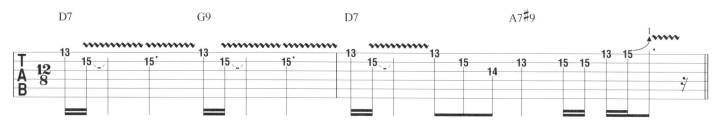

Key of A

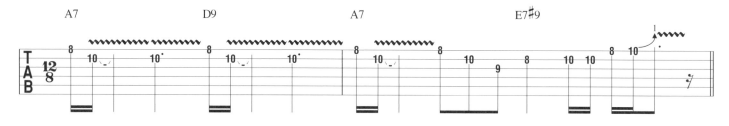

Key of G

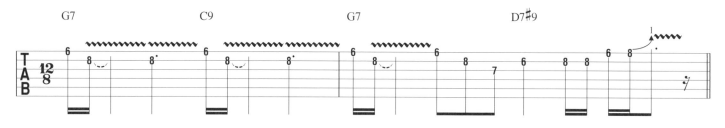

Turnaround 40
Texas Blues X

Stevie took "pride" and "joy" in seamlessly transitioning from the bass notes of the V chord in a chorus to the turnaround in a song that could be played as a complete, unaccompanied composition.

Key of A

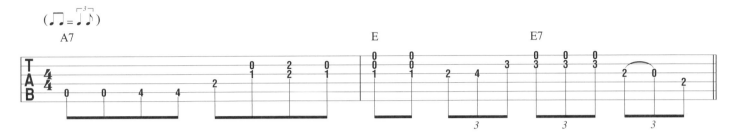

Key of G

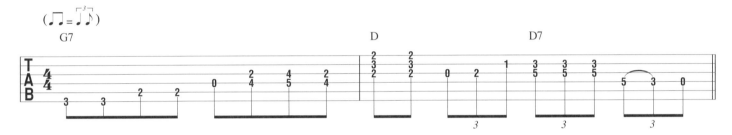

Key of E

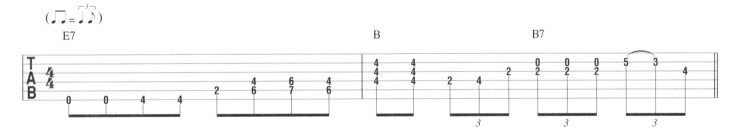

Key of C

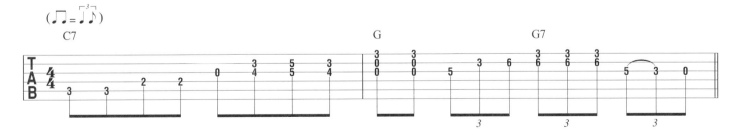

Turnaround 41
Jazz Blues I

Electric jazz guitar does not literally begin with Charlie Christian (1916–1942), but his enormous influence on the genre, beginning in the early 1940s with Benny Goodman's band, can hardly be exaggerated. Many of his up-tempo 12-bar blues performances resolve to the I chord in the last bar of the turnaround.

Key of C

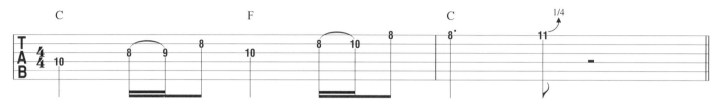

Key of A

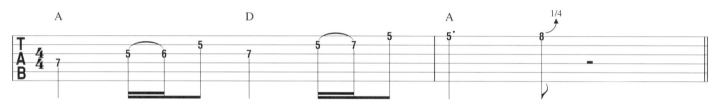

Key of G

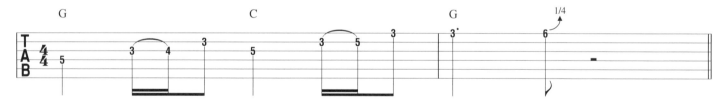

Key of E

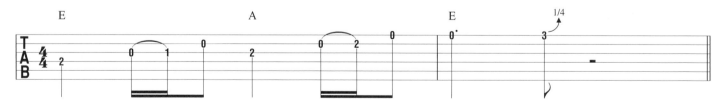

Turnaround 42
Jazz Blues II

Jimmy Shirley (1913–1989) is an unsung hero of swing guitar from the 1940s. In the 1950s, he hopped to jump blues and rock 'n' roll and recorded into the 1970s. *China Boy* (1975) was his first album as a leader.

Key of A

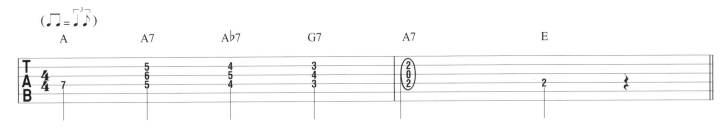

Key of G

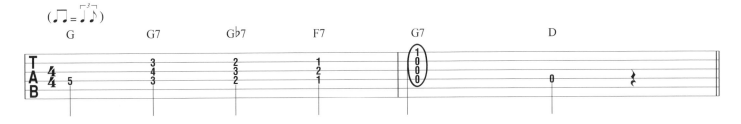

Key of C

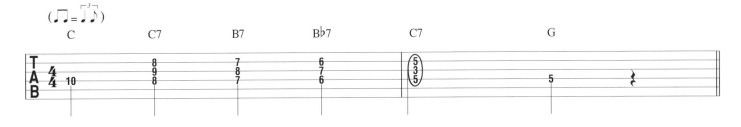

Key of D

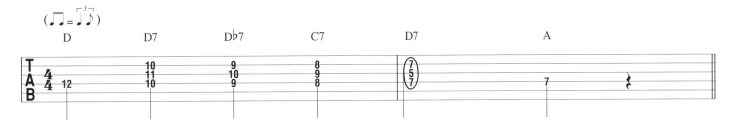

Turnaround 43
Jazz Blues III

Lloyd "Tiny" Grimes (1916–1989) made his legendary name in swing, bebop, boogie, and even rock 'n' roll on the 4-string tenor guitar; but fear not, his fleet forays translate well to the 6-string. The numerous luminaries he backed range from Art Tatum to Billie Holiday, Charlie Parker to Screamin' Jay Hawkins. In addition, he performed at Alan Freed's first Moondog Coronation Ball in 1952, believed by many to be the first rock 'n' roll concert.

In the first measure of each turnaround, notice the inclusion of the cool ♭5th "blue note" on the "and" of beat 2. It has been hailed by some as the defining sound of 20th century music.

Key of C

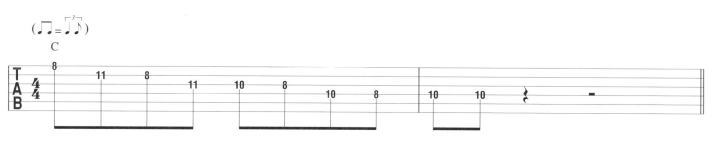

Key of A

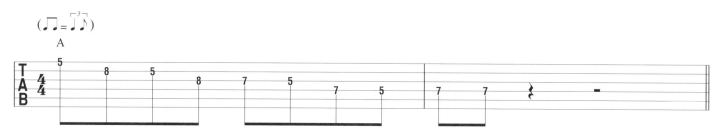

Key of G

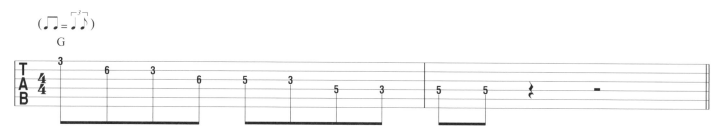

Key of E

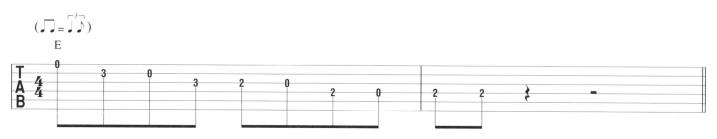

Turnaround 44
Jazz Blues IV

Kenny Burrell (1931–) is arguably the greatest exponent of jazzy blues guitar. He has had a long, illustrious career since the early 1950s, including his collaborations with the late Hammond B-3 virtuoso Jimmy Smith (a must-hear for blues guitarists). As opposed to many of his peers, he eschews gratuitous speed, instead going for finesse and choice note selection.

Key of G

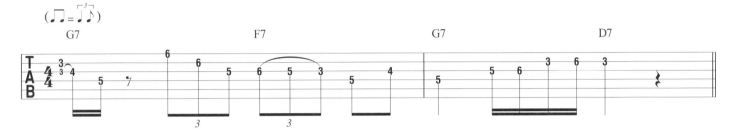

Key of A

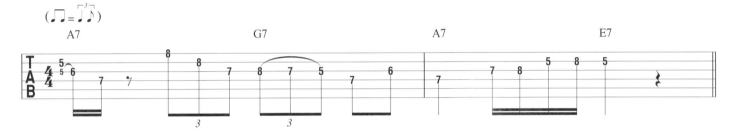

Key of C

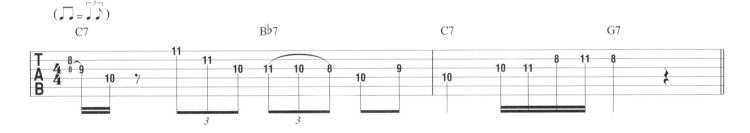

Key of E

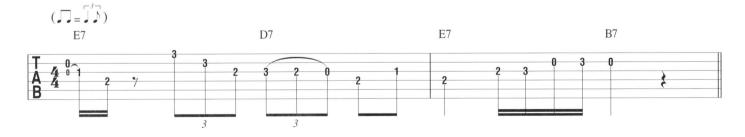

Turnaround 45
Jazz Blues V

A contemporary of Kenny Burrell with a deep love and knowledge of the blues was Joe Pass (1929–1994). Besides being a virtuoso single-string soloist, Pass was a master at playing unaccompanied solo guitar. Both jazz and blues songs fell easily from his fingers and featured chord melody and single-note lines interspersed with comp chords. Observe this jazzy I–VI–ii–V chord progression.

Key of C

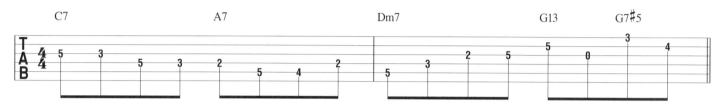

Key of A

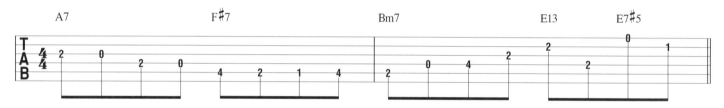

Key of G

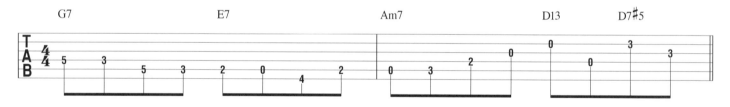

Key of E

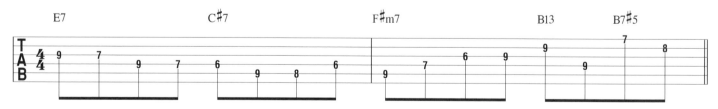

Turnaround 46
Jazz Blues VI

Avoiding the straight eighth notes he frequently embraced, Joe Pass creates an elegant turnaround emphasizing the important chord tones in a I–vi–ii–V progression.

Key of F

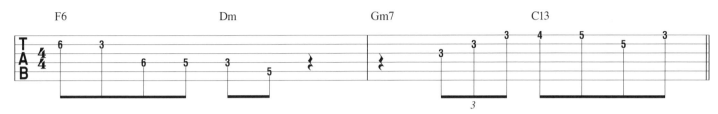

Key of G

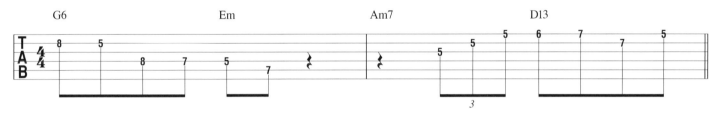

Key of A

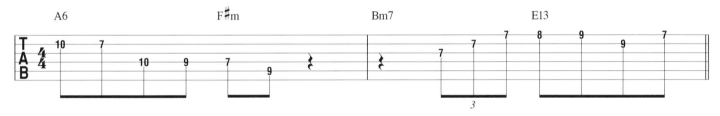

Key of C

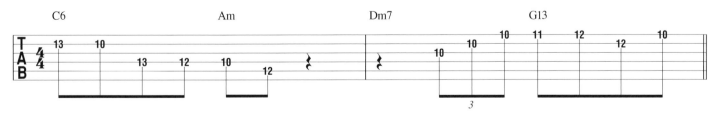

TURNAROUND 47
Jazz Blues VII

As can be seen, Joe Pass, along with many other jazz guitarists, was keen on seamlessly outlining the chord changes in his turnarounds. Be it known to all that broken chords and arpeggios are the jazz guitarist's stock in trade.

Key of F

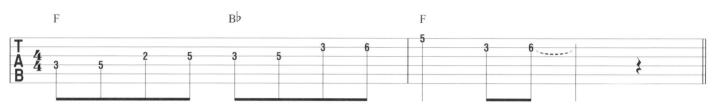

Key of G

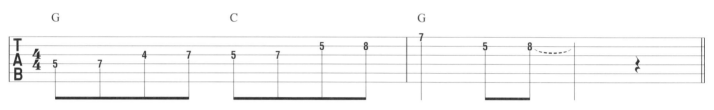

Key of A

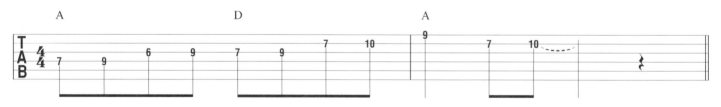

Key of C

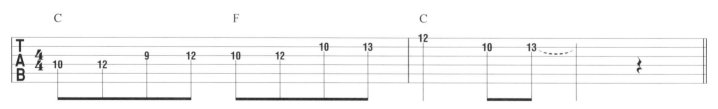

Turnaround 48
Jazz Blues VIII

Blues and blues-rock guitarists tend to play classic blues-scale runs that resolve to the root of the V chord in minor-key blues. However, jazz-blues guitarists, such as Pass, are just as likely to outline the chords in minor keys as they are wont to do in major keys.

Key of Cm

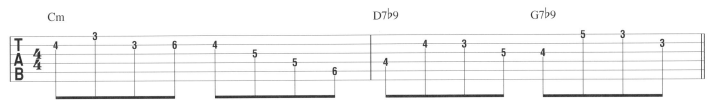

Key of Am

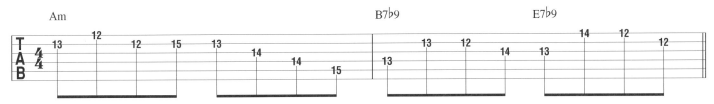

Key of Gm

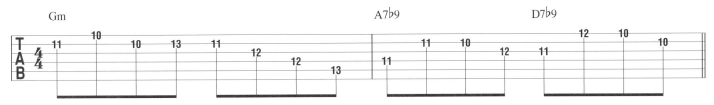

Key of Em

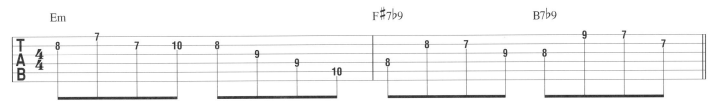

Turnaround 49
Jazz Blues IX

The lineage of jazz guitar legends, from Charlie Christian to Wes Montgomery, ultimately leads to George "Bad" Benson (1943–). Like his illustrious forebears, he can plunge deep into the blues with no apologies needed! As the turnaround remains on the dominant I chord (a dominant 13th in this case), Benson mines related A scales for their melodic gems, including the ever-popular A minor pentatonic in measure 2.

Key of A

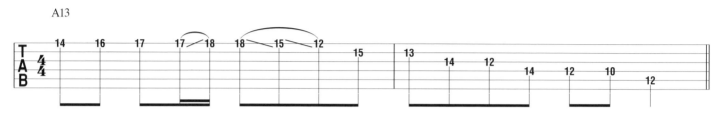

Key of G

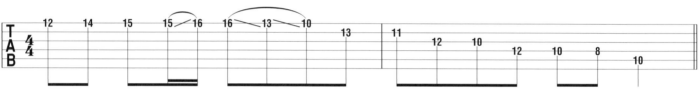

Key of F

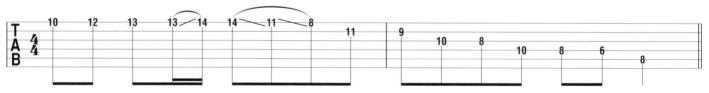

Key of E

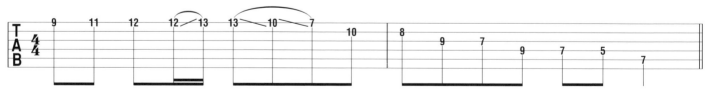

TURNAROUND 50
Jazz Blues X

It seems appropriate for the last jazz-blues turnaround to be from George Benson. It also features the most challenging phrasing as he darts in and around the changes. Notice how he uses the upper positions of the blues scale with intelligent emphasis on the gritty ♭5th (E♭ in the first example, D♭ in the second example, etc.) for poignant musical tension.

Key of A

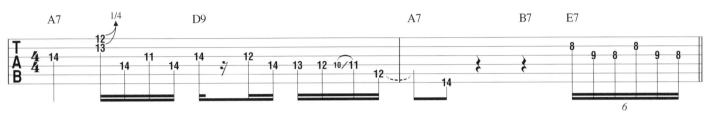

Key of G

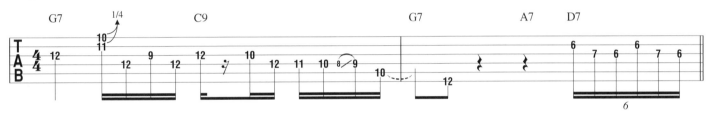

Key of F

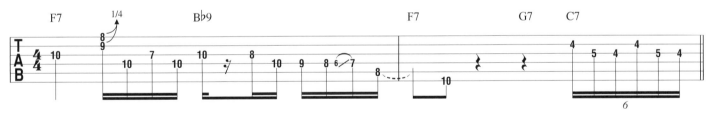

Key of E

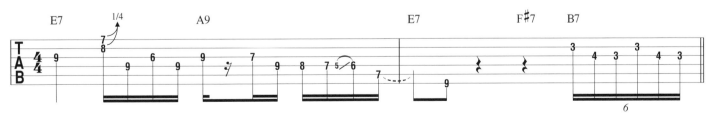

RHYTHM TAB LEGEND

Rhythm Tab is a form of notation that adds rhythmic values to the traditional tab staff.

TABLATURE graphically represents the guitar fingerboard. Each horizontal line represents a string, and each number represents a fret. Rhythmic values are shown using ovals, stems, and dots.

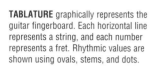

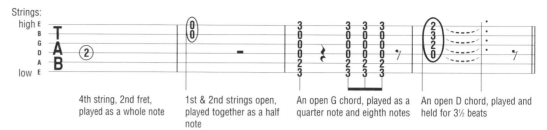

Strings:
high E
B
G
D
A
low E

4th string, 2nd fret, played as a whole note

1st & 2nd strings open, played together as a half note

An open G chord, played as a quarter note and eighth notes

An open D chord, played and held for 3½ beats

Definitions for Special Guitar Notation

HALF-STEP BEND: Strike the note and bend up 1/2 step.

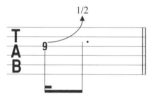

WHOLE-STEP BEND: Strike the note and bend up one step.

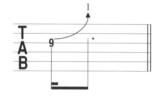

SLIGHT (MICROTONE) BEND: Strike the note and bend up 1/4 step.

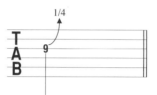

BEND AND RELEASE: Strike the note and bend up as indicated, then release back to the original note. Only the first note is struck.

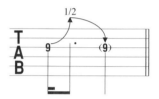

PRE-BEND: Bend the note as indicated, then strike it.

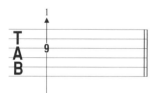

GRACE NOTE PRE-BEND AND RELEASE: Bend the note as indicated. Strike it and release the bend back to the original note.

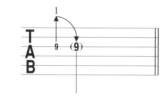

UNISON BEND: Strike the two notes simultaneously and bend the lower note up to the pitch of the higher.

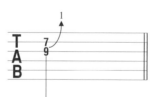

HOLD BEND: While sustaining bent note, strike note on different string.

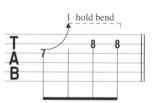

VIBRATO: The string is vibrated by rapidly bending and releasing the note with the fretting hand.

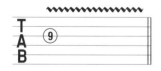

WIDE VIBRATO: The pitch is varied to a greater degree by vibrating with the fretting hand.

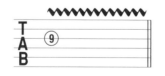

HAMMER-ON: Strike the first (lower) note with one finger, then sound the higher note (on the same string) with another finger by fretting it without picking.

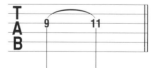

PULL-OFF: Place both fingers on the notes to be sounded. Strike the first note and without picking, pull the finger off to sound the second (lower) note.

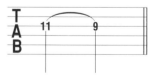

HAMMER FROM NOWHERE: Sound note(s) by hammering with fret hand finger only.

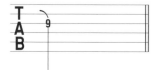

GRACE NOTE SLUR: Strike the note and immediately hammer-on (or pull-off) as indicated.

GRACE NOTE SLUR (CLUSTER): Strike the notes and immediately hammer-on (or pull-off) as indicated.

LEGATO SLIDE: Strike the first note and then slide the same fret-hand finger up or down to the second note. The second note is not struck.

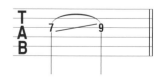

SHIFT SLIDE: Same as legato slide, except the second note is struck.

GRACE NOTE SLIDE: Quickly slide into the note from below or above.

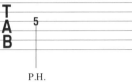

TRILL: Very rapidly alternate between the notes indicated by continuously hammering on and pulling off.

TAPPING: Hammer ("tap") the fret indicated with the pick-hand index or middle finger and pull off to the note fretted by the fret hand.

NATURAL HARMONIC: Strike the note while the fret-hand lightly touches the string directly over the fret indicated.

Harm.

PINCH HARMONIC: The note is fretted normally and a harmonic is produced by adding the edge of the thumb or the tip of the index finger of the pick hand to the normal pick attack.

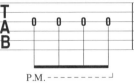

P.H.

HARP HARMONIC: The note is fretted normally and a harmonic is produced by gently resting the pick hand's index finger directly above the indicated fret (in parentheses) while the pick hand's thumb or pick assists by plucking the appropriate string.

H.H.

PICK SCRAPE: The edge of the pick is rubbed down (or up) the string, producing a scratchy sound.

P.S.

MUFFLED STRINGS: A percussive sound is produced by laying the fret hand across the string(s) without depressing, and striking them with the pick hand.

PALM MUTING: The note is partially muted by the pick hand lightly touching the string(s) just before the bridge.

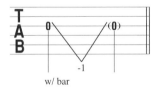

P.M. - - - - - - - - -

RAKE: Drag the pick across the strings indicated with a single motion.

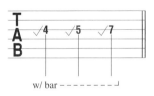

rake - ⌐

TREMOLO PICKING: The note is picked as rapidly and continuously as possible.

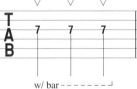

ARPEGGIATE: Play the notes of the chord indicated by quickly rolling them from bottom to top.

VIBRATO BAR DIVE AND RETURN: The pitch of the note or chord is dropped a specified number of steps (in rhythm), then returned to the original pitch.

VIBRATO BAR SCOOP: Depress the bar just before striking the note, then quickly release the bar.

VIBRATO BAR DIP: Strike the note and then immediately drop a specified number of steps, then release back to the original pitch.

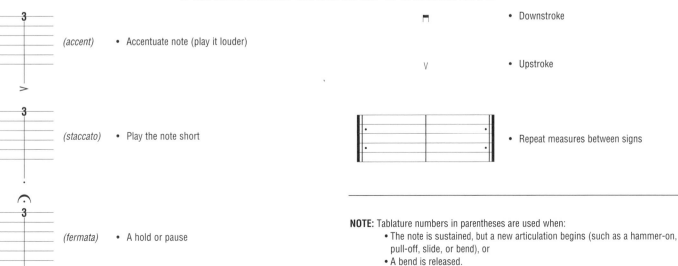

Additional Musical Definitions

(accent) • Accentuate note (play it louder)

(staccato) • Play the note short

(fermata) • A hold or pause

• Downstroke

∨ • Upstroke

• Repeat measures between signs

NOTE: Tablature numbers in parentheses are used when:
• The note is sustained, but a new articulation begins (such as a hammer-on, pull-off, slide, or bend), or
• A bend is released.
• A note sustains while crossing from one staff to another.

FIRST 50

The First 50 series steers new players in the right direction. These books contain easy to intermediate arrangements for must-know songs. Each arrangement is simple and streamlined, yet still captures the essence of the tune.

First 50 Blues Songs You Should Play on Guitar

All Your Love (I Miss Loving) • Bad to the Bone • Born Under a Bad Sign • Dust My Broom • Hoodoo Man Blues • I'm Your Hoochie Coochie Man • Killing Floor • Little Red Rooster • Love Struck Baby • Pride and Joy • Smoking Gun • Still Got the Blues • The Thrill Is Gone • Tuff Enuff • You Shook Me • and many more.

00235790 Guitar **$14.99**

First 50 Christmas Carols You Should Play on Guitar

Angels We Have Heard on High • Away in a Manger • Coventry Carol • The First Noel • God Rest Ye Merry, Gentlemen • Good King Wenceslas • The Holly and the Ivy • Jingle Bells • O Christmas Tree • O Come, All Ye Faithful • Silent Night • The Twelve Days of Christmas • Up on the Housetop • We Wish You a Merry Christmas • What Child Is This? • and more.

00236224 Guitar **$12.99**

First 50 Christmas Songs You Should Play on Guitar

All I Want for Christmas Is My Two Front Teeth • Blue Christmas • The Christmas Song (Chestnuts Roasting on an Open Fire) • Do You Want to Build a Snowman? • Feliz Navidad • Happy Xmas (War Is Over) • I'll Be Home for Christmas • Mary, Did You Know? • Rudolph the Red-Nosed Reindeer • Santa Baby • Silent Night • White Christmas • Winter Wonderland • and more.

00147009 Guitar **$14.99**

First 50 Classical Pieces You Should Play on Guitar

This collection includes compositions by J.S. Bach, Augustin Barrios, Matteo Carcassi, Domenico Scarlatti, Fernando Sor, Francisco Tárrega, Robert de Visée, Antonio Vivaldi and many more.

00155414 Solo Guitar **$14.99**

First 50 Folk Songs You Should Play on Guitar

Amazing Grace • Down by the Riverside • Home on the Range • I've Been Working on the Railroad • Kumbaya • Man of Constant Sorrow • Nobody Knows the Trouble I've Seen • Oh! Susanna • She'll Be Comin' 'Round the Mountain • This Little Light of Mine • When the Saints Go Marching In • The Yellow Rose of Texas • and more.

00235868 Guitar **$14.99**

First 50 Jazz Standards You Should Play on Guitar

All the Things You Are • Body and Soul • Don't Get Around Much Anymore • Fly Me to the Moon (In Other Words) • The Girl from Ipanema (Garota De Ipanema) • I Got Rhythm • Laura • Misty • Night and Day • Satin Doll • Summertime • When I Fall in Love • and more.

00198594 Solo Guitar **$14.99**

First 50 Rock Songs You Should Play on Electric Guitar

All Along the Watchtower • Beat It • Born to Be Wild • Brown Eyed Girl • Cocaine • Detroit Rock City • Hallelujah • (I Can't Get No) Satisfaction • Iron Man • Oh, Pretty Woman • Pride and Joy • Seven Nation Army • Should I Stay or Should I Go • Smells like Teen Spirit • Smoke on the Water • When I Come Around • Wild Thing • You Really Got Me • and more.

00131159 Guitar **$14.99**

First 50 Songs You Should Fingerpick on Guitar

Annie's Song • Blackbird • The Boxer • Classical Gas • Dust in the Wind • Fire and Rain • Greensleeves • Hell Hound on My Trail • Is There Anybody Out There? • Julia • Puff the Magic Dragon • Road Trippin' • Shape of My Heart • Tears in Heaven • Time in a Bottle • Vincent (Starry Starry Night) • The Wind • and more.

00149269 Solo Guitar **$14.99**

First 50 Songs You Should Play on Acoustic Guitar

Against the Wind • Barely Breathing • Boulevard of Broken Dreams • Champagne Supernova • Crazy Little Thing Called Love • Every Rose Has Its Thorn • Fast Car • Free Fallin' • Ho Hey • I Won't Give Up • Layla • Let Her Go • Mean • One • Ring of Fire • Signs • Stairway to Heaven • Trouble • Wagon Wheel • Wish You Were Here • Yellow • Yesterday • and more.

00131209 Guitar **$14.99**

First 50 Songs You Should Strum on Guitar

American Pie • Blowin' in the Wind • Daughter • Good Riddance (Time of Your Life) • Hey, Soul Sister • Home • I Will Wait • Losing My Religion • Mrs. Robinson • No Woman No Cry • Peaceful Easy Feeling • Rocky Mountain High • Sweet Caroline • Teardrops on My Guitar • Wonderful Tonight • You're Still the One • and more.

00148996 Guitar **$14.99**

Prices, content and availability subject to change without notice.

www.halleonard.com